MAN MADE MARVELS

DANNY PEARSON

Badger Publishing Limited
Oldmedow Road,
Hardwick Industrial Estate,
King's Lynn PE30 4JJ
Telephone: 01553 816083

www.badgerlearning.co.uk

2 4 6 8 10 9 7 5 3 1

Man Made Marvels ISBN 978-1-78837-661-7

Text © Danny Pearson

Complete work © Badger Publishing Limited 2022

All rights reserved. No part of this publication may be reproduced, stored in any form or by any means mechanical, electronic, recording or otherwise without the prior permission of the publisher.

The right of Danny Pearson to be identified as author of this work has been asserted by them in accordance with the Copyright, Designs and Patents Act 1988.

Commissioning Editor: Sarah Rudd
Copyeditor: Carrie Lewis
Designer: Adam Wilmott

Cover Image: Shutterstock/Aleksandr Artt, Shutterstock/RoseRodionova
Page 4: Shutterstock/WitR
Page 5: Shutterstock/Mountains Hunter
Page 6: Alamy/Bill Grant
Page 7: Shutterstock/Ivan Soto Cobos, Shutterstock/travelview, Shutterstock/mbrand86, Shutterstock/gnanistock, Shutterstock/Bildagentur Zoonar GmbH, Shutterstock/Yulia_B
Page 8: Shutterstock/GagliardiPhotography, Shutterstock/zosel
Page 9: Shutterstock/f11photo
Page 10: Zhangzhugang via Wikimedia Commons
Page 11: Zhu difeng via Wikimedia Commons
Page 12: Shutterstock/GuoZhongHua
Page 13: Shutterstock/SAKhanPhotography
Page 14: Shutterstock/TonyV3112
Page 15: Shutterstock/f11photo
Page 16: Shutterstock/inProgressImaging
Page 17: Shutterstock/Andrew Ring
Page 18: Shutterstock/mkos83
Page 19: Shutterstock/Sean Pavone, Shutterstock/S.Borisov, Shutterstock/Tatiana Popovs
Page 20: Shutterstock/Yuangeng Zhang
Page 21: Shutterstock/Jim W Kasom
Page 22: Shutterstock/GUDKOV ANDREY
Page 23: Shutterstock/Nicole Kwiatkowski
Page 24: Shutterstock/Stockbym and Shutterstock/MC MEDIASTUDIO
Page 25: Shutterstock/Theerasak Namkampa
Page 26: Shutterstock/Dziajda and Shutterstock/ever
Page 27: Shutterstock/Dima Zel
Page 28: Shutterstock/Digital Storm
Page 29: Shutterstock/Corona Borealis Studio

Every effort has been made to contact copyright holders of material reproduced in this book. Any omissions will be rectified in subsequent printings if notice is given to the publisher.

MAN-MADE MARVELS

Contents

1. Ancient Marvels	4
2. Modern Marvels	13
3. Bridges and Tunnels	18
4. Inspiration From Nature	21
5. What's Next?	26
Glossary	30
Questions	31
Index	32

1. ANCIENT MARVELS

Words **highlighted in this colour** are in the glossary on page 30

Ancient **marvels** from around the world give us clues about the past. It's quite surprising what our **ancestors** were capable of without modern technology to help them.

Pyramids of Giza, Egypt

One of the most famous and ancient man-made marvels are the Egyptian pyramids, with the oldest dating back to around 2600BC.

The Pyramids of Giza would have originally been gleaming white in colour, with smooth sides and golden caps. The largest of these pyramids, The Great Pyramid of Giza, was built using 2.3 million large blocks of stone, weighing over 5.4 million tonnes in total.

WOW! facts

The Great Pyramid wa the tallest man-made structure in the world f more than 3800 years

The Great Sphinx, Egypt

Nearby to the Pyramids of Giza is the Great Sphinx, named after a mythical creature with the head of a man and the body of a lion. The Great Sphinx is the oldest known statue in Egypt and one of the most recognisable in the world, with 14.7 million visitors a year.

The statue is made from a single piece of **limestone**, measuring 20 metres tall and 73 metres long.

It is thought to have taken 100 workers over three years to build and that the face is modelled on the ruler of the time, Pharaoh Khafre.

Aztec pyramids

The Egyptians weren't the only **civilisation** to build great pyramids. The Aztecs built many pyramid-shaped temples between the 12th and 16th centuries.

In fact, the largest pyramid in the world is in Cholula, Mexico. It is 55 metres high, and its base covers a massive 182,000 square metres – you could fit two Buckingham Palaces inside it!

It had been hidden from view for many years by the growth of trees and plants. The Spanish built a church on top, having no idea what lay beneath.

Pyramids around the World

Here are more examples of man-made pyramid structures that can be found on our planet.

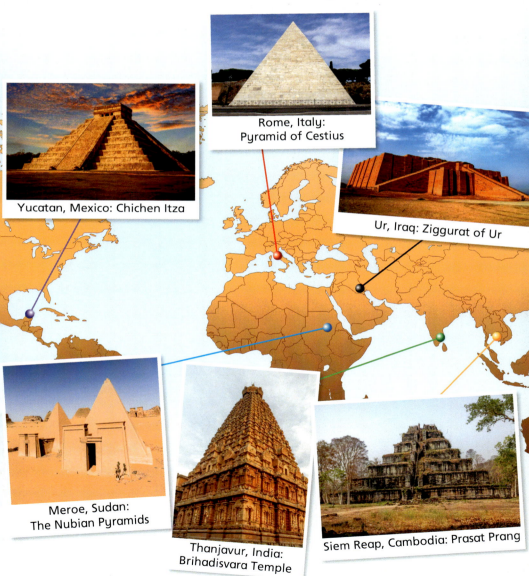

Rome, Italy: Pyramid of Cestius

Yucatan, Mexico: Chichen Itza

Ur, Iraq: Ziggurat of Ur

Meroe, Sudan: The Nubian Pyramids

Thanjavur, India: Brihadisvara Temple

Siem Reap, Cambodia: Prasat Prang

Modern day pyramids

Although it's not as ancient as the others, there is even a pyramid located in the USA. It is called Luxor, and is a 30-storey hotel and casino in Las Vegas.

In 1989, the Louvre pyramid was completed in Paris, France. It was built as an entrance to the Louvre Museum, the most visited museum in the world. It is home to many famous paintings, including the famous Mona Lisa.

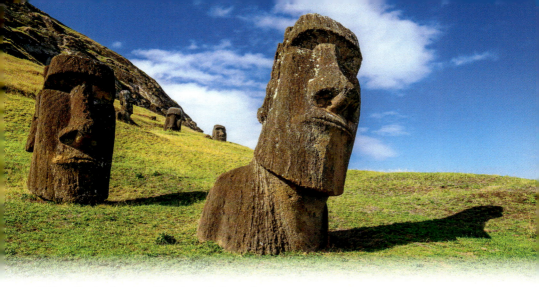

Moai statues, Easter Island

The moai statues are some of the most mysterious man-made marvels on the planet. There are 887 stone statues, the biggest weighing 74 tonnes and standing over nine metres tall.

The statues were built between the years 1400 and 1650 by the people living on the island, who were known as the Rapanui. It remains a mystery as to how the islanders managed to move such large stones across the four miles from the quarry to where they sit today.

The Easter Island heads do have bodies. Most photos show them buried up to their necks so we only see the top part.

Longyou Caves, China

The Longyou Caves are a system of 24 man-made caves that were discovered by accident in 1992 by local farmers when they decided to drain several ponds.

The caves date back to 200BC but there are no records of them being built or why. They remain a complete mystery and still baffle historians to this day.

The Great Wall of China

The Great Wall of China is the longest man-made structure in the world. The total of all sections, including those that have since disappeared, add up to 13,170 miles long. This is half the length of the **equator**!

The wall is over 2300 years old and probably needed around one million people for its construction. 400,000 labourers died and some are thought to be buried in the wall's foundations. It is sometimes called 'the longest cemetery on earth'.

The Great Wall of China is a very popular tourist attraction, with an average of ten million people visiting each year. One year, a single section alone attracted 63 million people!

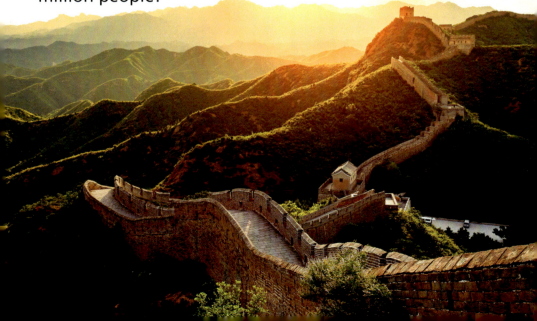

The Forbidden City, China

The Forbidden City was built during the Ming **dynasty** and is the world's largest **imperial** palace at 7.2 million square metres. It includes 980 buildings which, in total, have a whopping 8728 rooms!

The city was known as 'forbidden' because in the past, people could not leave or enter without permission from the emperor.

WOW! facts

If you visit the Forbidden City, you will notice there are no birds on the roofs. This is because they have been designed to make it impossible for birds to land on them.

2. MODERN MARVELS

New materials and building techniques mean that builders are able to make structures that are bigger, better and taller than ever before.

Burj Khalifa, Dubai
The current tallest building in the world is the Burj Khalifa at 828 metres high. It is three times the height of the Eiffel Tower in Paris.

The top of the Burj Khalifa can be seen from up to 60 miles away.

Shanghai Tower, China

The Shanghai Tower in Shanghai stands at 632 metres and took seven years to build, opening in 2010. Not only is it an extraordinary building but its elevators are also a genius of engineering. Made by Mitsubushi, they are the fastest in the world, travelling at 46 miles per hour.

WOW! facts

Up to 16,000 people can live and work inside the Shanghai Tower at any one time.

Walt Disney Concert Hall, USA

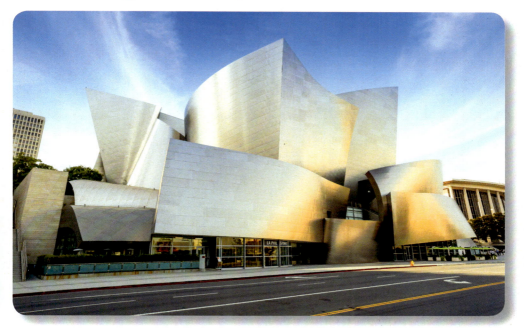

The Walt Disney Concert Hall in Los Angeles was completed in 2003 and cost around £218 million. It seats 2265 people and is one of the finest concert halls in the world.

WOW! facts

The sunlight glare off the stainless steel walls caused nearby apartments and pavements to reach a huge 60 degrees Celsius! It even caused traffic accidents, so some of the walls had to be sanded down in 2005 to stop the glare.

Amazing stays

These high-rise apartment buildings are the most glamorous in the world, housing the rich and famous.

Central Park Tower, New York, USA

Central Park Tower was built in 2021 and is the tallest apartment building in the world, standing at 472.4 metres. It is located on 'Billionaires' Row', where each apartment costs tens of millions of pounds. It overlooks New York's most famous landmarks, such as Central Park, the Empire State Building, and the Statue of Liberty.

The Shard, London, England

The Shard is 309.6 metres tall, and it contains a hotel, luxury apartments, a spa, a restaurant and 44 elevators. It is the tallest building in England, and it overlooks London's iconic landmarks, including Tower Bridge, the London Eye, and Houses of Parliament.

WOW! facts

95 per cent of the construction materials used to build The Shard are recycled.

Palm Islands, Dubai

The Palm Islands are a set of man-made islands formed by **dredging** the sea bed. The whole project cost an enormous £9.5 billion!

Although this man-made marvel may look beautiful, it has had a hugely negative impact on the local **environment**. Coral reefs have been destroyed, marine life is threatened and beaches are **eroding**.

3. BRIDGES AND TUNNELS

People are travelling more than ever before and **innovative** structures are needed to support modern travellers.

Tower Bridge, England

One of most famous bridges in the world, Tower Bridge took eight years to build and was opened in 1894. It can open and lift up to allow tall ships to sail through, which happens about 800 times a year.

In 1952, an unbelievable incident took place. A watchman failed to warn drivers that the bridge was about to open. A bus was halfway across when the bridge started to lift up. The quick-thinking driver sped up and managed to leap the gap without anyone getting hurt! He was awarded for his driving skills and bravery.

WOW! facts
In 1951, Frank Miller flew a plane through Tower Bridge because his 13-year-old son dared him to. He was fined £100.

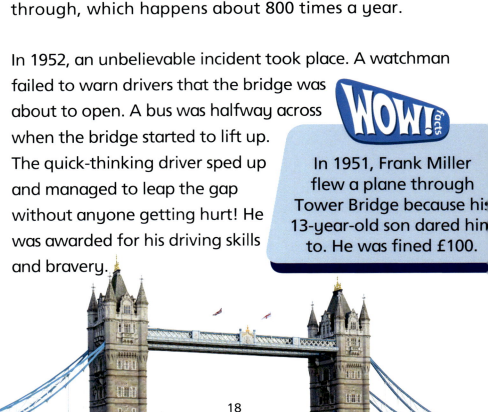

Akashi-Kaikyo Bridge, Japan took 12 years to construct and is 3900 metres long – this could fit a queue of 450 London buses! It is made from 305,000 kilometres of wire cabling and is designed to withstand earthquakes and high winds.

The Ponte Vecchio Bridge, Florence, Italy has held shops and houses on it since the 13th century. It was decided in 1545 that only goldsmiths and jewellers could sell their goods here, mainly because the ruling Medici family hated the smell of rotting meat given off by the butchers!

The Laerdal Tunnel, Norway is the world's longest road tunnel at over 15 miles long. It has been used to study driver psychology, and lights have now been placed in areas to help reduce driver tiredness and **claustrophobia**.

Guoliang Tunnel, China

Before this amazing tunnel was built the only way to reach the village of Guoliang was a dangerous path, known as the 'sky ladder', carved into the side of the mountain.

In 1972, a group of 13 villagers decided to dig a tunnel and began work with hammers and chisels. It was finished in 1977, measuring 1200 metres long, and cars could finally reach Guoliang.

This man-made marvel has become a popular tourist attraction not just because of its amazing story but also for its terrifying dips, twists and turns!

4. INSPIRATION FROM NATURE

WOW! facts
Some of the oldest known living bridges are over 500 years old.

Living bridges, India

These bridges, found in Meghalaya, India, are known as 'living bridges'. Meghalaya is one of the wettest places on Earth, making it impossible to use regular building materials. The local people have worked with nature by guiding roots of trees over rivers and valleys, but it takes many years for the bridges to form.

Treetop houses, New Guinea

The Korowai tribe have been living in the Indonesian Rainforest for thousands of years. They have mastered the art of building homes high up in the trees.

The Korowai tribe build their houses between 15 and 50 metres up. This protects them from slave traders and cannibals, but also helps them to avoid insects, wild animals and what they believe to be evil spirits in the forest below.

Eden Project, England

This enormous structure in Cornwall cost over £140 million to build. The giant greenhouses are made from special inflatable plastic cells, which house over 1000 varieties of plant in Mediterranean and tropical climates. This is the closest you will come to walking in a jungle in the UK!

The Eden Project is a man-made marvel that has many other uses. It regularly holds musical performances and has been used as a location for a James Bond film. It even holds the World Pasty Championships every year!

Gardens by the Bay, Singapore

The creators of this enormous nature park in Singapore were inspired by nature to help transform its 'garden city' to a 'city in a garden'. It looks like something straight from a science fiction film.

Bosco Verticale, Italy

Architects are looking at ways of combining outdoor living with inner city areas. One way of doing this is to create vertical forests.

These two residential towers built in Milan contain nearly 900 trees between them.

Svalbard Global Seed Vault, Norway

On a remote island, halfway between mainland Norway and the North Pole, is the Svalbard Global Seed Vault.

It is also known as the 'doomsday vault' as it protects the seeds from **extinction**. The vault has been built deep inside a mountain so the thick rock and permafrost will keep the seed samples frozen, even if the power is cut.

It currently contains around 860,000 seed samples, including 'cheesytoes', 'Asian pigeonwings' and 'zombie pea', but can hold up to 2.5 billion samples if needed.

5. WHAT'S NEXT?

Humans are now creating their own landscapes. They are also exploring ways to build in new environments.

Tropical Island Resort, Germany

What happens if you live miles away from the coast, but you want to experience the seaside? That's no problem if you live in central Germany. Here, they have created an entire beach resort miles away from the coast.

This huge dome, originally built to house a modern airship, is the largest free-standing dome in the world. It contains a huge indoor rainforest, made from over 30,000 trees. It also has a 200 metre long man-made beach and an artificial sea that stays at a warm 26 degrees Celsius all year round.

Living in space

We have seen how humans can create different environments here on Earth, but would we be able to live on other planets?

Humans are already living in space using the International Space Station, which was launched in 1998. The structure is over 100 metres long and contains six sleeping areas, two bathrooms and a gym. Astronauts must exercise for at least two hours a day, so their muscles don't waste away in zero-gravity.

The International Space Station is probably the most complex and difficult man-made marvel that has ever been created. So far…

The International Space Station circles around the world every 90 minutes, travelling at 17,500 miles per hour, which gives the crew 16 sunrises and sunsets a day.

Living on Mars

Plans are being made for humans to visit Mars in the near future.

Scientists recreated what it could be like to live and work on Mars in a testing facility, called the MARS-500 complex, built here on Earth. Crews of volunteers were locked in for up to 520 days. The results from these experiments will help us to learn more about what life on Mars might be like and how to cope with it.

An illustration of how human living quarters could look on Mars.

The future of humans

Humans have built some incredible marvels throughout history. This book has shown only a few examples of what we have managed to achieve and build, from the mysterious Longyou Caves to the International Space Station.

There are many exciting possibilities for man-made marvels of the future, such as:
- an elevator into space
- a transatlantic tunnel
- floating cities
- asteroid mining
- artificial forests

What marvels do you think humans will come up with next?

GLOSSARY

ancestor — a relative that came before you, usually a long time ago

claustrophobia — the fear of small spaces

dredging — taking material from the bottom of a body of water

dynasty — rulers who belong to the same royal family for generations

environment — the type of place that surrounds us, such as the air, water and the soil

equator — the imaginary line that circles around the middle of Earth, halfway between the North and South poles

eroding — to wear away or eat into

extinction — when there is no more of that species left alive in the world

imperial — relating to an emperor or empire

innovative — to propose or introduce new ways of thinking and make inventive changes

limestone — a type of sedimentary rock formed over

Questions

Name three countries where pyramids can be found *(pages 4-7)*

What year were the Longyou Caves discovered? *(page 10)*

When was Tower Bridge, in London, first opened? *(page 18)*

How many trees are on the Bosco Verticale? *(page 24)*

In what country would you find the Global Seed Vault? *(page 25)*

How many bathrooms are there on the International Space Station? *(page 27)*

INDEX

Akashi-Kaikyo bridge 19
Bosco Verticale 24
Burj Khalifa 13
Central Park Tower 16
China 10-12, 14, 20
Cholula 6
Dubai 13, 17
Easter Island 9
Eden Project 23
Egypt 4, 5
Eiffel Tower 13
Empire State Building 16
England 16, 18, 23
equator 11
Forbidden City 12
France 8
Gardens by the Bay 24
Germany 26
Great Sphinx 5
Great Wall of China 11
Guoliang Tunnel 20
India 21
International Space Centre 27, 29
Italy 19, 24
Japan 19
Korowai tribe 22
Laerdal Tunnel 19
living bridges 21
Longyou Caves 10, 29
Louvre 8
Luxor 8
Mars 28
Mexico 6
Ming dynasty 12
moai statues 9
New Guinea 22
Norway 19, 25
Palm Islands 17
pharaohs 5
Ponte Vecchio 19
pyramids 4-8
Pyramids of Giza 4, 5
Shanghai Tower 14
Singapore 24
Svalbard Global Seed Vault 25
The Shard 16
Tower Bridge 16, 18
treetop houses 22
Tropical Island Resort 26
USA 8, 15, 16
Walt Disney Concert Hall 15